P9-CBX-947

FOOL'S GOLD

FOOL'S GOLD

SHORTER POEMS

Norman Schaefer

Norman Schaefer

La Alameda Press :: Albuquerque

Grateful acknowledgement is made to Bob Arnold, editor of Longhouse,
who published some of these poems in two chapbooks:
Little Sierra Nevada Poems and A *Dog in Love Howls in Rhyme*.
Also thanks to Jerry Reddan, printer extraordinaire of Tangram,
who first issued the four poems on the back cover as a small broadside.

Cover painting: "Awakening" by John Schaefer
24 inches x 24 inches
oil and wax on wood panel

ISBN: 978-1-888809-66-4

Library of Congress Control Number: 2013944728

La Alameda Press
9636 Guadalupe Trail NW
Albuquerque, New Mexico 87114

for Jacqueline

PREFACE

I HAD WANTED TO WRITE SOME SHORT POEMS FOR A LONG TIME, and after reading Mary Barnard's translations of Sappho, I began writing some of my own. That was in 2001. I called the manuscript *Fool's Gold*.

I spent nearly as much time reading poetry during this project as I did writing it, and I learned some big lessons: "The natural object is always the adequate symbol" (Ezra Pound); "To learn the pine, go to the pine" (Bashō); "A poem is made of words and not words" (William Carlos Williams); "Boil it down, but boil it with a cold blue flame" (Kenneth Rexroth); and "The first duty of the poet is to name things properly" (Sam Hamill). I didn't know it then, but after ten years of writing poetry—most of it not very good—I was starting over again.

I tried to write poetry in *Fool's Gold* that was direct and clear and with minimum decoration. Precisely selected nouns and verbs will free a poem from the need of most modifiers. The power of the image and metaphor is what counts.

Fool's Gold is a collection of artifacts of nearly a decade of my life. There are many kinds of poems. The ones I like the best are about the Sierra Nevada and being in love. I hope you will find some that you like.

Norman Schaefer

Once it was a man's world.
Then, thankfully,
Audrey Hepburn arrived.

Clouds cover the stars over Mt. Clarence King
and darkness comes incomprehensible.
I can't explain anything tonight.

In dreams I defeated
all the great heavyweights,
but when I fought Sonny Liston
I was an egg against a stone.

Falling out of love,
a woman's body,
once as light as a feather
is the heaviest thing in the world.

As a poet I was born
in the fetal position.
Will I ever stand erect?

A perfect capital V
in bold italic
flying over the Sacramento River.

Enjoying the big view
from North Palisade,
here for a little while
above it all.

When lovers get married,
sometimes a husband and wife
are all that are left.

Mountaineering in the Sierra Nevada
gives my life rigor,
but hopefully not mortis.

Who is a more
gracious host
than an old Indian?

Although I'm a vegetarian,
I still like being
on top of the food chain,
so I eat a little turkey
during the holidays.

The trail through the mountains forked,
but the moon followed us both
when we went our separate ways.

Everywhere tears have fallen.
Grief is the dew
at daybreak.

The blood I give these
mosquitoes in July
won't help them when
it freezes in September.

Was it a dream then
when we climbed Matterhorn Peak?
Only the cold wind remains,
blowing down from Horse Creek Pass.

A politician is always there
when he needs us.

Heaven also grieves when lovers part.
By tens and thousands
the stars go out.

When I realized that astrology
was leading me astray,
I changed to fortune cookies
and overnight my life got better.

The older we get
the farther we walk
into the forest for wood.

Nights alone.
I don't know what I hate more:
hours of dark
or the pale rose of day.

Last year pictures of her
meant everything. Yesterday
I threw them in the fire.

There will be no pitter-patter
of rat's feet on the roof tonight.
Lucy, the cat, has left it in the kitchen.

Saigyō says there's joy
in loneliness.
So does Bashō.
Loneliness must be different
in Japan.

In the mountains seasons pass.
History happens elsewhere.

A hermit thrush
breaks out in song.
How opera began.

I've ground my molars down
to flat old stumps.
Shame, blame, and regret
in every dream.

If you want to ski
the John Muir Trail,
it's better to start with
a small state first
like Rhode Island.

When I lied to her,
I felt like an egg
in mid-air.

She was a gentle lover.
Once or twice
in her tenderness
she nearly killed me with love.

I've forgotten when the clock
on the bookcase stopped,
but I think I've been 54
for about 2½ years.

Sometimes under the covers at night
she would stay awake
and help me with my poems.

Will the night come
when I'm sure
I've made a mistake?

Slowly, slowly,
this sorrow will pass,
and here to help
is the evening star.

Whoever believes money can't buy happiness
hasn't bought a Mont-bell 20°-rated,
goose down, zipperless, 16 oz. sleeping bag.

My poems are only
a few inches long,
but how vast the mountains.

Last night I was lost in the dark,
but at dawn the daylight
came back for me.

Americans should be careful
not to have children
eighteen years before a war.

All I want to be
is a bear
who knows where everything is
in the mountains
and how to get there.

For some Buddhists
it's always catch and release
whether it's earwigs, flies,
cockroaches, or trout.

Even if the river dries up,
there will be a little stream
to float away on.

What has the butterfly
lost in the meadow
that it keeps looking for?

When I was 21 I decided to study Zen,
but I threw the year away
wandering alone in the Sierra Nevada
and along the beaches and bays
of the Northern California coast.

We are what we eat,
which for Sophia Loren
means spaghetti.

A pipit sings at dawn
by an unnamed lake.
Today looks pretty good
for me too.

Today I picked up
a piece of litter downtown
and put it in the trash.
Boy, the things I do
for the city of Davis.

Dawn put a rosy arm around my shoulder,
looked into my eyes, and without a word
showed me the way up Bear Creek Spire.

I may never be able to write like
the ancient Chinese masters,
but if I stop eating I can look like them.

On Plum Lane
the wife is the only one
who doesn't know.

What luck in a lifetime to see
an albino robin!

Fields of yellow mustard
in Vacaville
are pods of gray whales
at Point Reyes.

After kindergarten
we played doctor in her closet,
but the next day she wouldn't speak to me.
Gretchen could be fickle at six.

Just like that
spring came to Yosemite
in a deep blue sky.

The esteemed leaf raker
works all morning
in a kitchen
cleaning an oven.

Wedges of geese
fly over Old Davis Road.
I honk the car horn back.

If you haven't stood on top of
the Black Kaweah at dawn
and looked east toward Mt. Whitney,
then north as far as Mt. Ritter,
you might be missing out on half your life.

An ant rides
across town
on the handle bar.

The left boot minus the heel
and a handful of dried bananas.
Fifty miles to go to the truck.

I've pulled a lot of weeds in my life,
and I still get excited when
one comes out with a little pop,
roots and all, on the first try.

Walking in Cold Canyon,
the stick I almost stepped on
coiled and rattled just in time.

Stars blossom at dusk,
first Arcturus, then Vega.
I might be next!

I thought it would
make me tough,
but four years of boxing
took all the fight out of me.

The Milky Way is my roof tonight.
A granite slab makes a floor.
The moon for a lamp and a breeze a broom.
Take off your shoes before coming in.

If we lived like the coyote,
we'd be content with small blessings,
a ground squirrel here, a jackrabbit there.

At a dry stream
in October
shapeless, weightless,
a bear drinks deep.

A view from Middle Palisade:
sunshine, blue sky, snowy peaks.
This is heaven.
You don't even have to check for ticks.

I'm almost six feet tall,
but certainly not in the eyes
of the waitress this morning
I forgot to tip.

After the blossoms have fallen,
there's nothing to talk about
but allergies.

I came to Little Five Lakes
to be alone for a while,
so this monsoon blew in
at just the right time.

2 A.M.,
I drink tea to help me sleep.
Each sip is a toast
to the wildflowers I love the most.

Sometimes it takes
many families joining hands
to hug a giant sequoia.

If Abraham Lincoln were alive today,
the only ID he'd need in an airport
would be a penny in his pocket.

A kind word,
well-aimed,
can warm a
winter's day.

To be free a while
from raking leaves and cutting wood.
I fill the truck with gas,
thinking of Big Sur.

Walking on the sandy stream bottom
inside those bits of twigs and leaves
is a caddisfly larva,
the inventor of the mobile home.

When I was twelve my girlfriend, Diana,
showed me her underarms,
and I wished mine had hair like hers.

This silence
on top of Mt. Humphreys
just about explains everything.

After reading the poetry of Hayden Carruth,
I know how the village fiddler feels
after listening to Paganini.

Mountains are a cold and icy place
for someone seeking
fame and fortune,
yet a haven
for an empty-handed wanderer.

On a moonlit boulder
the shadow of a bear.

Still, at night before I go to sleep,
I ask God, if there is one,
to save my soul, if I have one.

When I soar
I catch on fire:
red-tailed hawk.

So happy after climbing Mt. Clarence King.
Swimming in a cold lake, singing,
laughing, jumping up and down —
that's the way to live.

Those years in my twenties
went through me like water
and I pissed them away.

A fly has landed on
my avocado sandwich.
But relax, there's plenty
for both of us.

The way a clump of poppies perks up
the whole county dump.

I have wandered
far and wide
in the Sierra Nevada,
but nothing like
the autumn wind tonight.

Unemployment hovers like a kestrel,
but it doesn't swoop this low.
Take no pity on this unskilled laborer.
If he had a Ph.D., he might not have a job.

Drinking from my
tin cup,
I swallowed the moon.

One lifetime a congressman,
the next ten a beggar.

Twelve years ago
I fell to my death on Mt. Russell.
I'm doing well,
but sometimes on Saturdays
I miss *Prairie Home Companion.*

An oak
will give its shade
to anyone.

How shocking it was to turn forty
when almost overnight
I no longer knew everything.

I wake up
rich in silver:
snow on lodgepole pines.

Zenobia said she liked my red hair
and for a hundred dollars
would be the date of my life.
Greater love hath no hooker.

One night asleep in the mountains
a large animal jumped on me
and grabbed my shoulders.
It was not a deer.

We should be like the bobcat
who is always ready.

Three flies
and a yellow jacket
dead in the tub.
Have I gone that long
without a bath?

Like father like son
the president talks of peace
with a mouthful of blood.

So pleased with my faded red hair,
still bright enough to attract a hummingbird.

I wish it were snow,
but cherry blossoms
are beautiful too
falling in misty rain.

Stars are seeds,
dawn the harvest.

When I saw Meryl Streep
in *Kramer vs. Kramer*,
I knew men and women
weren't created equal.

A trout leaps
in mountain air.
The sky is bluer
for the brave.

Sometimes a cricket
is all you need
for a night to exist.

Higher than a hawk
I climb in the sky
and take a breath
on the summit of
Norman Clyde Peak.

War logs a forest,
taking the best trees.

You told me you couldn't hear
the call of the wild,
so I gave you my ears.

The horse packer remembers
to drink upstream
from the herd.

Winters are cold on
the Sawtooth Ridge,
but not cold enough to remarry.

The bear mauled him
until there was nothing left.
Then he ran into the woods
like a child, a new man.

The long, long
faces of bananas
longing for Ecuador.

I was only seven when
Floyd Patterson winked at me,
but for a moment I too was
the heavyweight champion of the world.

We eat and in turn
are eaten. No one
gets off Earth alive.

On a granite slab
in Yosemite
as smooth as marble
I rolled a quarter a hundred yards.

President Bush has a
big ranch in Texas,
but real cowboys have patience
and a cool eye.

For the island of Australia
to become a continent,
it was a dream come true.

I'm out of water,
but not out of love
for the primroses in bloom
on Milestone Mountain.

When you fought Sugar Ray Robinson,
just showing up at the weigh-in
was half the losing battle.

Lighting the peaks,
the moon shines down
on everything alike.
One touch of nature
makes the whole world kin.

I grow older
and more and more women
can kick my ass.

It's not so funny
the spider has the fly
in stitches.

An awakened mind
is said to be priceless,
but how can it compare
with the view from Mt. Sill?

I burned for Barbara
like a bonfire on the beach
by Bodega Bay.
That's too many Bs, but too bad.

Cherries blossom
in the capital
even for the White House.

A poet wants money,
not praise.

What pleasure: a full tank
of gas in the truck
and California Highway 1
in front of me.

I loved and feared the bear that night
as I did my mother and father
when I was a little boy.

We go out together
hunting deer:
a bow and arrow.

I do pull-ups to build muscle,
but Lao-tzu did nothing
and grew as strong as water.

Egret chicks eagerly await
their mother's return
with a regurgitated meal
of fish, mice, crayfish, and frogs.

I am a bioregional poet.
My bioregion is the California Sierra Nevada.
Posted: No Trespassing.
Squatters are warned.

Even a gentle breeze
gives us the jitters:
quaking aspens.

Health and long life:
our forests want it too.

My idea of paradise is
a platter of my mother's French toast
on top of Half Dome
and Etta James to share it with.

The history of the United States:
how would they tell it,
the sun and moon?

In every epic poem
there is a haiku
trying to get out.

How do you learn
a range of mountains?
With an open heart and your feet too.

Fragrant after the rain,
sky pilots bloom on Forester Pass.
When I smelled the blue flowers,
I danced all the way to Cedar Grove.

If you're for a clearcut,
you're against a forest.

This one
dogwood in bloom
is all the spring I need.

Axe splitting logs
in the woods.
The hills are alive
with the sound of music.

Was it me who once picked daffodils
late at night from a neighbor's garden
because he was too cheap to buy them
for his lover? It was.

After the bear attack
Orion looked down
from the sky
as if nothing had happened.

A Buddhist
washes everything
on the gentle cycle.

Drinking icy snow water
from Taboose Creek —
a cavity!

Every third week in February
almonds blossom as white as snow.
Spring has never needed
more than one or two colors.

I sit on my cushion twice each day
and get only this aching back.
Clearly I don't have the spine for Zen.

Please, aphids,
just eat
the neighbor's roses.

What have I learned
bouldering at Indian Rock?
Free rock shoes
always give you blisters.

For a turtle
any day's a good day
for a slow start.

After trying my whole life
to get my feet on the ground,
I finally let go of myself
and floated up in the sky.

And what is the sea horse's
question?

Not easy to forget:
wind and moonlight
on top of Mt. Ritter.

I'm getting too old to want
my afternoons to go faster.
Even while waiting in line
at the DMV.

My love affair with Cynthia
was no different from the others.
First it spread like wildfire,
but then it ran out of fuel
and went out.

When you wake up in Mendocino
with the sun in your eyes,
already your day's complete.

How vivid the stars are
after a brush with death.

Computer illiterate,
I can no longer fulfill
any meaningful bureaucratic role.
I have become a California condor
in the Age of Information.

Sooner or later
a crow shows up
wherever you are.

"I don't like listening to Mozart anymore,
but who else is there?" Carolyn asked.
"How about John Lee Hooker?"

Gazing quietly from Clouds Rest,
hikers aren't strangers anymore.

Chaco sandals, a goose down bag,
lightweight fleece, and a
Gore Tex rain jacket:
other possessions may lead you astray.

I hope I'll always be
young at heart
despite growing older
in some other places.

A view of the Kaweahs
from Sawtooth Peak:
wealth enough for one afternoon.

What has become of
the Great Mountaineer?
Today he only looks at wildflowers.

A good morning: I raked the last
of the leaves and pruned the roses.
Then on the radio an old country
favorite: "I Bought the Shoes that
Walked Right Out on Me".

When Clay beat Liston
in Miami, it was if Jonah
had swallowed the whale.

The rosy-finches on Mt. Whitney
know me from way back.
If I leave out some cashews,
they'll come for sure.

Thin ice:
some of Mono Creek
will be staying here tonight.

Today I wasted another
balmy February afternoon
smelling spring's first blossoms.
Thank you, California.

In Tehipite Valley
there are rattlesnakes and bears,
but good luck abounds.

I've been told there's
a cloud of butterflies
in front of my eyes
if only I could see them.

I thought Pavarotti could sing,
then I heard the Merced River.

After eating the fermented
pyracantha berries,
robins stagger on the grass
too drunk to fly.

Read all morning in my sleeping bag,
then climbed Cathedral Peak.
I'm a lucky man,
but someone has to be.

A willow
always knows
where the water is.

Trout bending a fly rod
and my father's face
in the mountain air.

When I climbed higher,
the two turkey vultures
soaring over Mt. Clark
were golden eagles.

Graffito in Death Valley:

Raindance Saturday
at Furnace Creek
weather permitting.

I'm never welcome,
but I smile anyway:
a dandelion.

Ah, to be lost
in the mountains
where no one else
can find you either.

Kay Wooden, eighty-five,
just moved into a nursing home.
"My worries are over. I'm stuck here."

What is the practice of Zen,
but peeling away pretension?
Even the Buddha, they say,
is still peeling somewhere.

Last night at Sam Mack Meadow
I sat so still my body disappeared.
My boots walked back to Glacier Lodge.

Moonlight and glaciers:
what more do I need tonight?

In the mirror
my sagging buttocks
remind me to fix
the pickup's flat tire.

Following the trail to East Lake,
I remember bringing my wife here
to climb Mt. Brewer.
We were married the day before
and thought our love would last forever.

Listening to Monk
hit the wrong notes.
The wrong notes are right.

Why shouldn't a giant sequoia die
when all the rest of us have to?

After all that chiseling,
it's good the woodpecker's bill
grows back.

When I crossed Pinchot Pass
under the first full
autumn moon,
I never felt like
I was walking in the dark.

Sometimes climbing a peak,
I'll stand on a ledge
and sing like Frank Sinatra.

One big storm
and the creek thinks
it's a river.

In Yosemite Valley
the leaves of bigleaf maples
turn yellow and red,
and after they have fallen
no end to the raking.

I'm fifty-five
and I still don't know
what women want.
Maybe it's shoes.

Fog is the breath
of mountains.
Clouds are dreams.

Hungry Packer Lake
mirrors the sky —
trout jumping out of a cloud.

Last night I became frantic
thinking I'd lost my shadow,
but then the moon rose
and I found it again.

The guitar that once played
"Purple Haze"
now only cries
when you pick it up.

When the snow melts,
Rae Lakes Basin
overflows with hikers.

Humans scream when chainsawed;
redwoods, too.

I'm not the person
I once was.
I have known this
all my life.

Snow falls endlessly.
Mountains and meadows sleep.
Only the tungsten mine
on Pine Creek stays awake.

Violence has broken out on my scalp
since I switched to Head and Shoulders.
Inadvertently I have started a lice civil war.

"I don't know why you go up there,"
my mother said. "Mountains are
no place for a person of breeding."

I have lived more than
twenty thousand days
and still no tomorrow.

Like walking into the mountains,
when you enter the world of poetry
you never completely come back.

There's a difference when you
find a bear in your tent
than one in your neighbor's.

Will you join me
in the moonlight tonight,
Bashō,
walking round and round
Little Claire Lake?

If we could think again
of wilderness as home
that would help.

An enlightened mind,
I can't conceive of one
unless it looks like
where I walked today:
Evolution Valley.

When you know you're a fool,
you can live in the world.

Even with all its awe
the Sierra Nevada
doesn't humble enough of us,
but bringing back the grizzly will.

Why is it the less
women look at me
the more I look at them?

Blisters on my feet, raccoons got my food,
sleeping bag soaked after slipping in a stream.
Hungry, dirty, too tired to talk in the parking lot,
I'll be back soon.

We should be wary of the camel
and anyone else who goes a week
without having a drink.

After living a month
in the mountains,
how strange to sleep in a room
without animals or stars.

The ex-boxer died,
speaking a language
only his wife could understand.

I knew I shouldn't,
but I said it anyway
and the fastest horses
couldn't catch my words.

One step into the wild
and the wild steps
into you.

Fence lizard,
why all those push-ups
in the hot sun?

Even if no lover comes,
I'll still have
the blue
Polemonium gardens
on Forester Pass.

My shelf of classics in the sixties:
Kerouac, Ginsberg, Rexroth, Snyder,
Suzuki, Muir, Bash , Thoreau,
and *The Tassajara Bread Book*.

The next time I hear
someone say "touchy-feely",
I'm reaching for my slingshot.

They call me a weed,
but then I bloom:
a hollyhock.

On this windy ridge
high above timberline
there's no place to camp.
So anywhere is good.

I may be long in the tooth
and have a face
only a mother could love,
but on a good day
this old heart can still spark.

This life,
how easy it seems
for the bright, cloudless moon.

Descending Arrow Peak,
I wish darkness came
later at night.

No one else has enough rockets
to aim at ours anymore.
Where is the Soviet Union
when we need them?

A swallow makes
its mud nest
one mouthful at a time.

When I didn't see Jacqueline in July or August,
I thought I never would.
Then late September she called
and the sky came back from far away.

Handsome in her twenties,
another thirty years
has made her beautiful.

When you're as old
as I am,
just thinking about
the length of the Muir Trail
can bring you to tears.

What should we call
the mayfly
that drifts into June?

When I trimmed the roses this morning,
I thought of Jacqueline
and burst into bloom again.

Quietly
like a firefly
I burn for her.

Pale crescent setting over Mt. Dana
while crickets sing. Mono Basin
does its best talking at night.

A strange democracy indeed
that says who you can
or cannot marry.

Will it only be in dreams
when Jacqueline and I
ever kiss?

Through a tear
in the tent:
the Pleiades.

I carried Jacqueline's groceries
five miles through the rain
because I wanted to prove to her
I could bring home the bacon.

A fly is happy
to land on any cowpie
in the pasture.

For her I would be
as true as the North Star.
Would she take advantage?

We drink a toast
to our hunger and thirst
and cut the long
December night in two.

Rainbow trout rest,
touching each other.

It's spring again in Giant Forest.
This must be Eden. Everything
has that just-created smell.

In boxing we learn
it's more blessed to give
than to receive.

As if it were mine:
reading and dozing
by Precipice Lake.

For so long I'd forgotten
the joys of love-making.
How wonderful again
to stand and deliver.

In Lone Pine
there isn't much to see,
but what you hear in the café
makes up for it.

When Jacqueline
said she loved me,
I quit jaywalking.

Daybreak at Lake Reflection,
a good time
to call it a day.

Once withering like a beetle-ridden pine,
now I have needles and cones.
Tonight I'll give Jacqueline
what I owe.

She is
my iris,
my lily,
my lake.

Better even than *A Chorus Line*:
sandhill cranes singing, dancing, bowing.

On the Middle Fork of the Kings River
Tehipite Dome is the only head
without a care.

A poet lives slowly.
What takes seconds to read
can take months to write.

Until now there's never been a woman
I'd walk more than a few steps to hell for,
but I'd walk halfway for Jacqueline
and probably a lot farther.
Don't laugh. That's a big improvement.

White dust
in a black bowl:
Milky Way.

How wonderful to live on
north Puget Sound,
the rain on the roof
just right for sleeping.

Every morning there are scars, wrinkles,
stubble, and the same yellow teeth.
Mirrors have always mistaken me
for someone else.

Jacqueline and I have decided
not to have an open relationship.
At our age who has the energy?

One kiss lights the quilt
and we cook all night
like baking bread.

Dog days in Port Townsend:
gentle breezes off the bay,
mostly blue sky,
70°.

The Olympics
may be more beautiful,
but the Sierra Nevada is my home range.
A migratory bird
returns to the same tree.

Folding the towels and sheets
and Jacqueline's skirts and sweaters,
what is nirvana but seeing
one thing through to the end?

White goop on my forehead.
What I get for admiring a crow.

"Breathe!" I say,
"Push! Push!"
to Split Mountain,
giving birth to the moon.

Ripe cherries
as they hang
become a pie.

All the deer have run off.
Do they think the moon shines brighter
at the other end of the meadow?

When I kissed my
mother's cold lips,
I learned how dead
dead was.

Humming a Tony Bennett melody
while scrambling over
Thunderbolt Pass,
I look back at North Palisade
where years ago I left my heart.

Wanted: chihuahua serial killer
for Tyler Street neighborhood.
Will provide .22 with silencer.

Floating downstream,
the empty wine bottle
is just another steelhead
to the Sol Duc.

The hen walks
through the mud
with her pants rolled up.

Darkest winter.
The sun has left
Port Townsend
for Mexico.

After so many seasons
mountaineering in the High Sierra,
I visit now for the lakes and flowers.
Perhaps inside a man somewhere
there is a woman.

Is it the sun
or a low carb diet
melting pounds off the snowman?

When I got knocked down six times,
I was Mike Tyson's sparring partner,
but then I woke up in Yosemite.

When I walked off the trail,
I was in the middle of nowhere
with everywhere to go.

Flies are welcome
at the Salal Café
and eat with some of
Port Townsend's best.

There wasn't any wood
for the stove,
so I heated the cabin
with Stevie Ray Vaughn.

Even an old man
would want to touch
Mt. Baker's white skin.

The pewee is named
for its song,
not for its size.

I haven't driven the Toyota pickup
for two weeks. This morning
I sense it's getting restless
for a ride up to Hurricane Ridge.

We hope we would
snitch on a senator
before we would a friend.

Why is it the dirtier
I get in the mountains,
the cleaner I feel?

I have grown older
and know what it is to appreciate
a bed in a motel.

A woman is only a woman,
a logger from Forks told me,
but a good Homelite is a chainsaw.

I've written about a lot of good places
in the Sierra Nevada,
but the best ones I've never mentioned.
You'll have to find them yourself.

Is this poem fool's gold
or a nugget at the bottom
of a clear stream?

Mouse told it to Deer,
who told it to Raven,
who told it to the forest.

Promise me
when I'm gone,
pines,
to grow tall
and have lots of kids.

Sometimes a car will start itself
for a little warmth
in a snowstorm.

What have I learned?
The gods are thieves.
If you sleep among bears,
hang your food.

Autumn snowfall:
even the nameless peaks
get decorated.

Sixty-one years:
the best I've had so far.
I wouldn't trade them for anything.
Certainly not the next sixty-one.

It takes time to learn a river
isn't just about water.

Dawn took my pen away.
Some things she said
you don't write about.

Norman Schaefer is the author of
The Sunny Top of California (La Alameda Press, 2010).
He lives in Port Townsend, Washington.

Set in Dante designed by Giovanni Mardersteig and first used to print Boccaccio's *Trattatello in Laude di Dante* in 1955 by the Officina Bodoni. "What the future of typography will be, nobody knows. But we who don't belong to the big industry believe that it is necessary to aim for the highest standard as a model for others, so that our crafts will not lose their importance. The art of printing should never die." The original type was cut by Charles Malin and based on types by Francesco Griffo, a fifteenth-century punchcutter who worked with Aldus Manutius in Venice.

Book design by JB Bryan

OTHER BOOKS FROM LA ALAMEDA PRESS

The Art of Love Miriam Sagan

Here on Earth Larry Goodell

Sojourner So to Speak Joseph Somoza

Chalkmarks on Stone Carol Moldaw

How Rain Records Its Alphabet John Tritica

Chaco Trilogy V.B. Price

Sofia Joan Logghe

Caws & Causeries Anselm Hollo

red table(S Mary Rising Higgins

Inch by Inch :: 45 Haiku by Issa
(translated by Nanao Sakaki)

Rue Wilson Monday Anselm Hollo

Again :: 1989-2000 Joanne Kyger

Ears on Fire Gary Mex Glazner

Red as a Lotus Lisa Gill

Freud by Other Means Gene Frumkin

Wild Form, Savage Grammar Andrew Schelling

Trilogy Pentti Saarikoski
(translated by Anselm Hollo)

Equivalence Shin Yu Pai

Beat Thing David Meltzer

Rag Trade Miriam Sagan

Snows Gone By James Koller

Point of No Return Anne Valley Fox

Home Among the Swinging Stars Jaime de Angulo
(edited by Stefan Hyner)

Outrider Anne Waldman

As If the World Really Mattered Art Goodtimes

Letters to Early Street Albert Flynn DeSilver

Skull Highway Lawrence Welsh

Road to the Cloud's House John Brandi & Renée Gregorio

Dark Enough Lisa Gill

Splitting Hard Ground Marilyn Stablein

Joe's New Religion John Orne Green

The Sunny Top of California Norman Schaefer

Vanishing Act Bruce Holsapple

Seeding the Cosmos John Brandi

From the Arapaho Songbook Andrew Schelling

Standing in Astonishment John Tritica

Hinge Trio Heller Levinson, Linda Lynch, Felino A. Soriano

Bone Horses Lesley Poling-Kempes

Aux Arcs Shin Yu Pai

www.laalamedapress.com